IBN BATTUTA

# Ibn Battuta

## THE JOURNEY OF A MEDIEVAL MUSLIM

Edoardo Albert

**KUBE**
PUBLISHING

*For my parents,*
*who travelled nearly as far*
*as Ibn Battuta.*

Ibn Battuta: The Journey of a Medieval Muslim

First published in England by Kube Publishing Ltd,
Markfield Conference Centre, Ratby Lane, Markfield,
Leicestershire LE67 9SY, United Kingdom
Tel: +44 (0) 1530 249230
Fax: +44 (0) 1530 249656
Website: www.kubepublishing.com
Email: info@kubepublishing.com

Design, typesetting, maps, patterns: Louis Mackay
Editor: Yosef Smyth

A Cataloguing-in-Publication Data record for this
Book is available from the British Library

ISBN 978-1-84774-047-2 paperback

Printed by Imak Ofset, Turkey

# Contents

# Maps

# Illustrations

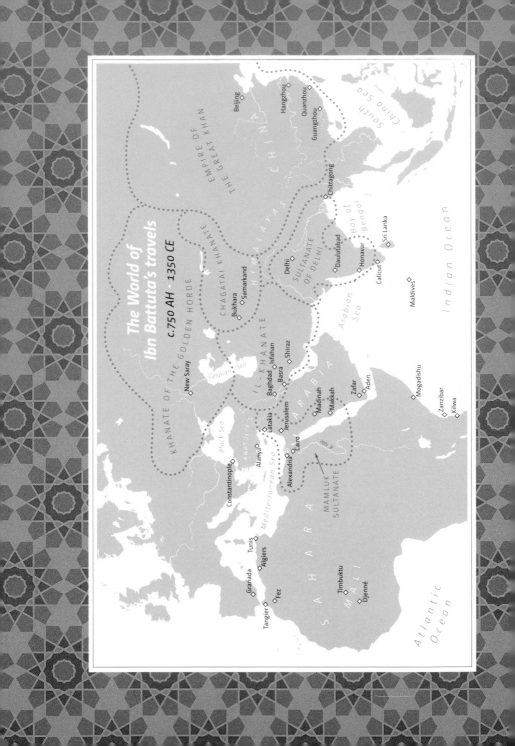

The World of
Ibn Battuta's travels
c.750 AH · 1350 CE

EMPIRE OF THE GREAT KHAN

KHANATE OF THE GOLDEN HORDE

CHAGATAI KHANATE

IL-KHANATE

SULTANATE OF DELHI

MAMLUK SULTANATE

CHINA

HIMALAYAS

ARABIA

SAHARA

MALI

South China Sea

Indian Ocean

Bay of Bengal

Arabian Sea

Caspian Sea

Black Sea

Mediterranean Sea

Atlantic Ocean

R. Nile

Beijing
Hangzhou
Quanzhou
Guangzhou
Chittagong
Daulatabad
Honavar
Delhi
Calicut
Sri Lanka
Maldives
Samarkand
Bukhara
New Saray
Isfahan
Shiraz
Baghdad
Basra
Jerusalem
Latakia
Alanya
Constantinople
Cairo
Alexandria
Madinah
Makkah
Zafar
Aden
Mogadishu
Zanzibar
Kilwa
Tunis
Algiers
Granada
Fez
Tangier
Timbuktu
Djenné

# Who was Ibn Battuta?

Ibn Battuta was a traveller. But he was no ordinary traveller. Between 1325 CE when he set off and 1354 CE when he finally returned home to stay, he went from Morocco to Makkah, up and down either side of the Red Sea, through Persia and Iraq, down the west coast of Africa, across Anatolia, into Russia and then down to India, across to China, back to North Africa and finally into the depths of the Sahara desert. He visited places that today would be in about 40 countries and travelled roughly 75,000 miles, going on foot, camel, horse, wagon, boat and even sled! He visited virtually every part of the world to which Islam had spread at the time. When Ibn Battuta returned to Morocco, the sultan, learning of his adventures, commissioned a young scholar named Ibn Juzayy to write a record of his travels. This literary genre, the *rihla* or book of travels, was well known in the Islamic world at the time. The *Book of Travels* of Ibn Battuta took two years to write, and was the longest and most detailed of all the North African books of travel.

In the *Rihla*, Ibn Juzayy records the worlds, particularly the political and social worlds, through which Ibn Battuta travelled in his 29 years on the road, as well as telling Ibn Battuta's adventures along the way. So the book is history and travelogue, a window into both the 14th century and one man's extraordinary life.

In the West, the obvious comparison to Ibn Battuta is Marco Polo. The Venetian died in 1324, the year before Ibn Battuta took to the road. By way of comparison, the Moroccan travelled much further than Marco Polo's 15,000 miles, and the Venetian spent 24 years on his travels compared to Ibn Battuta's 29. But neither traveller wrote the accounts that would make them famous. In the case of Marco Polo, his travels were written by Rustichello da Pisa while both men were prisoners in Genoa – presumably it helped fill the time. However, Ibn Battuta went to many places that Marco Polo did not reach, and his broad curiosity about human life – from the reluctance of Maldivian Muslim women to cover their breasts to witchfinding in India – provides insights into a huge variety of different customs. While there are other important travelogues by Muslim writers, most notably Ibn Fadlan's account of his journey to the Volga Vikings in the 10th century, no one else went as far or

North Africa and the western Mediterranean. from the Catalan Atlas dated 1375CE.

12

stayed away for longer. As such Ibn Battuta's *Book of Travels* provides an unparalleled insight into the 14th century.

So why did Ibn Battuta travel so far and so long? For him, the first and most important reason was the road. For most of his adult life, Ibn Battuta could not resist the desire to see what lay beyond the horizon. However, travel was hardly unusual in his time, particularly for educated Muslims or those seeking to become educated. The two foremost Muslim thinkers of the 11th and 12th centuries, Ibn Sina and Al Ghazali, travelled widely, seeking teachers, students and patrons. As a scholar of Islamic law, Ibn Battuta found a ready welcome in the Muslim courts he visited, and his experiences give us a vivid portrait of the cosmopolitan, almost globalised political culture that had been created within the Islamic world by the 14th century. Being a world of absolute monarchs though, he also lets us see the arbitrary cruelty inflicted by some of these rulers on their subjects.

While today we read Ibn Sina and Al Ghazali for their thought and their lives, Ibn Battuta is remembered for his insatiable wanderlust. Ibn Battuta gives us a fascinating window into what the world was once like. He is also a charming and funny guide. Let's set out, and follow him on his journey.

Leaving Tangier.

CHAPTER ONE
# A World to the East

Ibn Battuta was born on 24 February 1304 in the city of
Tangier in modern-day Morocco. All we know of his early
life is what he tells us in his book, and he doesn't say much.
His full name, which according to Muslim custom was very
long, was Abu 'Abdallah (father of Abdullah) Muhammad
(his first name) ibn 'Abdallah (son of Abdullah) ibn
Muhammad (grandson of Muhammad) ibn Ibrahim al-
Luwati (great-grandson of Ibrahim, from the Berber tribe
of Luwata) ibn Battuta (his family name). He was born
into a family that specialised in Islamic law. Ibn Battuta had
relatives who were *faqihs* (lawyers) and *qadis* (judges), so
it was natural that he should receive a similar education.

Ibn Battuta's education started with him learning to
read, write and memorise the Qur'an, the holy book of
Islam. By the age of 10 or 12 he would probably have
known it off by heart. For many boys of that time, school
ended at that point and they went on to learn a trade by
apprenticeship, or to help their father on their family
farm, but for Ibn Battuta it was only beginning. For the
next eight years he learned Arabic grammar, theology,
logic, Islamic law, rhetoric (the art of public speaking) and
**Hadith** from the best teachers in Tangier.

Along with his studies, the young Ibn Battuta was

learning to be a scholar and a gentleman. To be an '*alim* and a member of the **ulama**, a man had to be polite as well as knowledgeable. Students were taught to show great respect for their elders and their teachers. Little did Ibn Battuta know it at the time, but he was acquiring the manners that would see him made welcome in the courts of kings throughout the Muslim world.

As he went through his teenage years, Ibn Battuta specialised in studying law or Shari'ah, with the intention of becoming a judge. It was at some point during these years of study that he began to dress like a lawyer, wearing a big turban, a cape with a hood that went over his head and shoulders, and a long gown with wide sleeves. He also grew his beard.

During his early years, Ibn Battuta was also introduced to Sufism. A Sufi is a Muslim who seeks direct experience of God through prayer and meditation. By the 14th century, Sufi orders – groups of Sufis under the guidance of a particular religious leader – were deeply embedded in Moroccan society.

### Education in the Muslim World

In Ibn Battuta's day teachers taught lessons either at their homes or at the nearest mosque. The best and brightest pupils were those who remembered the most and asked the best questions. Those who wanted to go on to teach a certain subject or a particular book would be tested orally by their teachers, and if they passed they would receive an *ijazah*, or certificate for teaching that book or subject. Since there were no written exams, cheating was impossible!

A madrasa.

With his studies completed, Ibn Battuta's eyes turned eastward. Morocco lay at the far west of the Islamic world with only the ocean beyond. It is incumbent upon every Muslim who is able to do so to make the pilgrimage to Makkah, and Ibn Battuta's first motive to travel lay in fulfilling that obligation. But he also knew that a vast swathe of Muslim countries stretched away from Morocco, far into the east. As a qualified judge of Islamic law, Ibn Battuta could expect to find employment in most of the places he visited but he would learn as he went just how many doors his legal skills would open for him.

**Hajj and the Five Pillars of Islam**

The religion of Islam has five 'pillars', or things every Muslim should do: declare faith in One God and the Prophet Muhammad, pray daily, give to charity, fast in Ramadan, and make pilgrimage to Makkah.

Ibn Battuta lived over 4,500 kilometres [3,000 miles] from Makkah and knew that it was best for him to make his pilgrimage while he was still young, strong, and in good health. In Ibn Battuta's day, pilgrims had to walk all the way to Makkah, or go by camel or horse or ship. It was difficult and dangerous, and could take months or even years. People who fell ill might treat themselves with herbal remedies, or hope to meet a doctor along the way.

*In his own words*

**" I left Tangier, my birthplace, on Thursday, 2nd Rajab, 725 [14 June 1325], at the age of 22, with the intention of making the Pilgrimage to the Holy House [at Makkah] and the Tomb of the Prophet [at Madinah]. I set out alone because I could find no companion to cheer the**

Pilgrims on the way to Makkah.

*way with friendly talk, and no group of travellers to associate with. But I was moved by an overwhelming feeling and a cherished desire since my childhood to visit those glorious holy places, so I made up my mind to leave all my friends and tear myself away from my home. As my parents were still alive, it was very difficult to part from them, and both they and I were very sad about it.* ”

Ibn Battuta travelled east soon meeting other travellers. Although North Africa was fairly peaceful at the time, thieves and highway robbers would not hesitate to rob anyone they could catch, so people usually travelled together when journeying from one town to another.

Since many Muslims made the pilgrimage, there were also well-established hajj routes and large hostels or resting places, called caravanserai, for pilgrims and other travellers to use. But the companionship of others could be heartbreaking too, as Ibn Battuta found out when his group reached Tunis.

*In his own words*

**" The residents of the city came out to meet the members of our party, and on all sides greetings and questions were exchanged, but not a soul greeted me because I didn't know anyone there. I felt so lonely that I could not keep back my tears, and wept bitterly. "**

However, Ibn Battuta was soon taken in by a kind companion and by the time he left Tunis, he had become so well known that he was appointed *qadi* of a caravan of pilgrims. In fact, as the caravan made its way east towards Makkah along the shores of the Mediterranean Sea, Ibn Battuta must have felt that

A caravanserai in Tunisia.

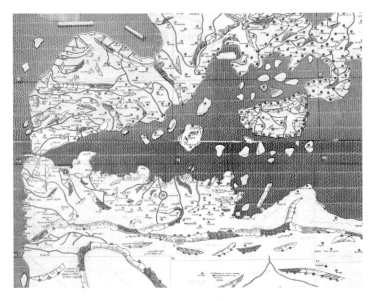

A detail of a 1928 German reproduction of a map made by al-Idrisi in 1154 CE, showing Tangier at the extreme left (lettering appears upside down).

things had very much improved for him. No longer the poor and lonely traveller who had left Tangier months before, not only was he a *qadi*, but he had earned enough money to marry the daughter of one of his fellow pilgrims. She was the first of several women that Ibn Battuta married during his travels.

Tunis lies nearly 1,500 kilometres [900 miles] east of Tangier. Ibn Battuta had already come a long way from home, but his travels were only just getting started.

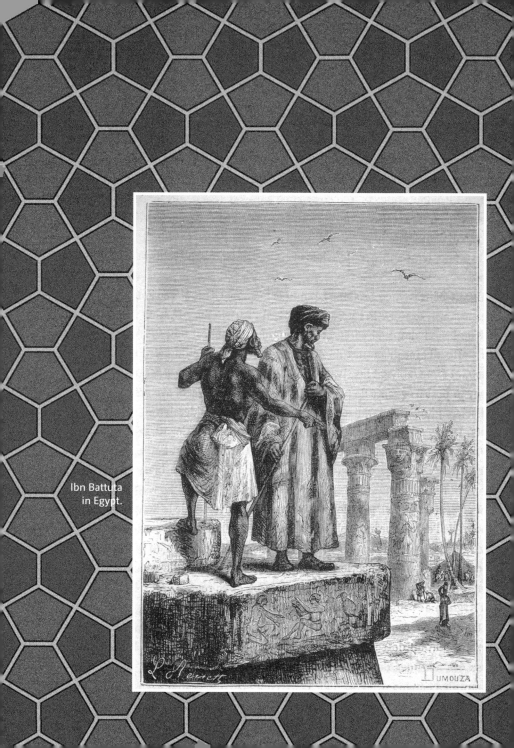

Ibn Battuta
in Egypt.

CHAPTER TWO

# Up the Nile

Sometime early in 1326, Ibn Battuta arrived in the port of
Alexandria, Egypt. He was a young man of 22 and Egypt
was one of the centres of the Islamic world, as well as being
the ancient home of the civilisation of the Pharaohs. The
first thing he mentions seeing was the famous Lighthouse,
one of the seven wonders of the ancient world. Though
once one of the tallest buildings in the world, it had been
damaged by earthquakes and Ibn Battuta reported that 'one
of its faces [was] in ruins'.

But ancient monuments were not the only things
Ibn Battuta went to see during his stay in Alexandria.
He also sought out holy men, Sufi shaykhs, or teachers,
as would be his practice wherever he travelled within
the Islamic world. One such **shaykh** was called Burhan
al-Din the Lame, who lived alone in the countryside.
Ibn Battuta stayed with him for three days, during which
the shaykh prophesied that Ibn Battuta would visit three
fellow sufis who lived in India, Sindh (modern-day
Pakistan) and China.

If that wasn't enough, while visiting another ascetic,
Shaykh al-Murshidi, Ibn Battuta had the prophecy
repeated in his dreams. While staying with the shaykh,
Ibn Battuta went to sleep on the roof of the shaykh's

**Seven Wonders of the Ancient World**

- The Great Pyramid of Giza
  (the only one that is still standing today)
- The Lighthouse of Alexandria that Ibn Battuta saw
- The Mausoleum at Halicarnassus
- The Colossus of Rhodes
- The Temple of Artemis in Ephesus
- The Statue of Zeus at his temple in Olympia, Greece
- The Hanging Gardens of Babylon

Illustration of the Lighthouse of Alexandria from *The Book of Wonders.*

house to escape the heat. He dreamed that he was 'on a great bird which was flying me towards Makkah, then to Yemen, then eastwards, and thereafter going towards the south, then flying far eastwards, and finally landing in a dark and green country, where it left me'. He told the dream to the shaykh who said it meant he would travel on, past Makkah, to India and China. What was more, Shaykh al-Murshidi also had a brother living in India whom Ibn Battuta was destined to meet, named Dilshad, who would save him from great danger.

Thereafter Ibn Battuta sailed along the River Nile to Cairo, the capital of Egypt and the largest city in the Islamic world. Over half a million people lived there when Ibn Battuta visited, drawn to the city by its power and its trade. In comparison, Ibn Battuta's home town of Tangier must have seemed a backwater, despite its status as a centre of trade and piracy.

" *The Egyptian Nile surpasses all rivers of the earth in sweetness of taste, length, and usefulness. No other river in the world can show such a continuous series of towns and villages along its banks, or a basin so intensely cultivated. It runs from south to north, contrary to all the other [great] rivers. One extraordinary thing about it is that it begins to rise in the extreme hot weather, at the time when rivers generally diminish and dry up...* "

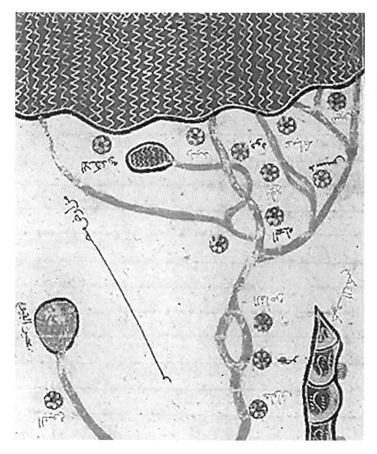

Detail showing the Nile Delta from a map by Al-Idrisi.

Cairo was home to the Mamluks, rulers of an empire that included much of modern Egypt, Palestine, Lebanon, Syria and Jordan. Its scholars were the finest in the Islamic world. And among its many wonders was the al-Mansuri Maristan, a huge hospital that impressed Ibn Battuta. For people could receive the best medical care of the time for free. No wonder people wanted to live there.

Ibn Battuta only stayed for a short time, choosing to continue with his travels and make for Makkah by travelling down the River Nile, across the desert and then catching a boat across the Red Sea. At least

Al-Azhar, Cairo, the most famous Islamic institution in Egypt and the second-oldest university in the world, was founded at first in 970 CE as a madrasa and drew scholars to its doors from far and wide.

that was his plan, and the most direct route. But as so often in his travels, the direct route would prove impossible, so Ibn Battuta would go the long way round. While the lands in these parts were well governed and generally safe for travellers, in one of the memorable asides that pepper the *Rihla* Ibn Battuta gives us a vivid insight into the particular difficulties of 14th-century travel.

*In his own words*

**❝ One of our halts was at Humaythira, a place infested with hyenas. All night long we kept driving them away, and indeed one got at my baggage, tore open one of the sacks, pulled out a bag of dates, and made off with it. We found the bag next morning, torn to pieces and with most of the contents eaten. ❞**

## The Mamluks

Mamluk comes from the word for 'property' in Arabic but the designated property were men: these were slaves. So what were slaves doing ruling an empire? The answer is that they used to be slaves. The origins of this caste of slave-soldiers in medieval Islam is obscure but by the 14th century the system was embedded across much of the Muslim world. In the realm ruled by the Mamluks – which at its height included present-day Egypt, the Levant and the Hejaz, the west coast of Saudi Arabia – slave boys were taken from largely Turkic and Circassian peoples, trained in the disciplines of war and Islam and isolated from the rest of the population. This produced an intensely loyal and very skilled military caste. The system had begun with the previous rulers of Egypt, the Ayyubids, who had needed extra soldiers. So they bought thousands of young boy slaves from Central Asia and Eastern Europe to train up and fight their wars. After a while, the slaves became very powerful – to the point that they decided they should be in charge!

Mounted Mamluks.

They overthrew the Ayyubids in 1250 but kept the name of Mamluks, and they continued to import slave boys from Central Asia and Eastern Europe to train up as soldiers. The most talented of them became commanders in the army, or amirs. Ordinary Egyptians, and even the Egyptian-born sons of Mamluks, were not permitted to become Mamluks. The system was successful in producing a stable ruling caste: the Mamluk Sultanate endured for over 250 years. It was ultimately overthrown by the Ottomans, who had created their own system of recruiting slave soldiers: their feared janissaries.

The holy city
of Makkah.

## CHAPTER THREE

# To Makkah and back

The port where Ibn Battuta had intended to catch a ship
across the Red Sea to reach Makkah was blocked because
of a rebellion, so he had to return to Cairo and try to take
another route. He decided to go northeast, via Damascus
in Syria, which also gave him the chance to visit many holy
places in Palestine. He went to see Hebron, where Prophets
Abraham, Isaac and Jacob and their wives were buried,
and Bethlehem, where Jesus was born. He also visited
Jerusalem, the third most holy city in Islam after Makkah
and Madinah, and home to the Dome of the Rock.

*In his own words*

**" The Dome of the Rock is a building of extraordinary
beauty, solidity, elegance, and uniqueness of shape... Both
inside and outside the decoration is so magnificent and
the workmanship so great that it defies description. Most
of it is covered with gold so that the eyes of whoever
gazes on its beauties are dazzled by its brilliance... "**

Pressing on, Ibn Battuta passed through Tripoli before
arriving in Damascus on 9 August 1326 (9 Ramadan 726).
It was already more than a year since he had left home and
Ibn Battuta still had not made it to Makkah. Damascus
was the Mamluk citadel in the east, and a huge army was
garrisoned there.

However, the city's Mamluk rulers, in particular Saif al-Din Tankiz who ruled there from 1313 to 1340, made the city a place of beauty as well as strength. The most beautiful of all its buildings was the Great Mosque, known as the Mosque of the Umayyads after its builders. The Great Mosque was also a great centre of learning and Ibn Battuta received *ijazah*s from some of the teachers there, certifying that he was able to teach the texts he had studied. But studies could not keep Ibn Battuta in one place for long, and after a month he set off again, joining the hajj caravan to Makkah.

It was 1,320 kilometres [820 miles] from Damascus to Madinah and it took the caravan about 50 days to cover the distance. On the evening the caravan arrived in Madinah Ibn Battuta and some travelling companions went to pray at the mosque where the Prophet Muhammad is buried, as well as the Caliphs Abu Bakr and 'Umar. He then went to visit the Cemetery of al-Baqi, where the Prophet's daughter Fatima and many other of his relatives and close Companions were laid to rest.

*" On this journey our stay at Madinah lasted four days. We used to spend every night in the illustrious mosque, where the people, after forming circles in the courtyard and lighting large numbers of candles, would pass the time either in reciting the Qur'an from volumes set on rests in front of them, or in intoning litanies, or in visiting the sanctuaries of the holy tomb. "*

The Prophet's Mosque and Tomb in Madinah.

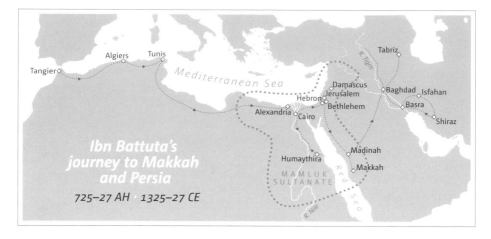

Ibn Battuta's journey to Makkah and Persia

725–27 AH · 1325–27 CE

Some days later, and a year and four months after setting out, Ibn Battuta arrived in Makkah, dressed in the plain white cloth of the pilgrim and saying:

What is Thy Command? I am here, O God!

What is Thy Command? I am here!

What is Thy Command? I am here!

Thou art without companion!

What is Thy Command? I am here!

*In his own words*

*" We kissed the holy Stone; we performed a prayer of two bowings at the Maqam Ibrahim and clung to the curtains of the Kaaba at the Multazam between the door and the black Stone, where prayer is answered; we drank of the water of Zamzam. "*

Now Ibn Battuta was a **hajji**, someone who had completed the pilgrimage to Makkah. The obvious thing would have been to return home. He had been gone for a year and a half, and he had already seen more of the world by his early twenties than most people would in their whole lives. But the words of the Egyptian Sheikh Burhan al-Din, who had interpreted his dream by saying that he would travel beyond Makkah, echoed in his mind when deciding what to do next.

Instead of going home to Morocco, Ibn Battuta set off with a caravan to Iraq and Persia.

Persia and Iraq were at the heart of the Islamic world but they were only just beginning to recover from the huge destruction and loss of life caused by the Mongol invasions between 1220 and 1260. But at least there were

The Mongol invasion of Baghdad.

### The Mongol invasions

In forty years the Mongol peoples, under the command of Genghis Khan, created the largest land empire the world has ever seen, stretching from China right across Asia and into the Middle East. Persia and Iraq were all but destroyed, with millions of people dying as the result of war and famine. Yet, by the time Ibn Battuta travelled through these lands, their Mongol overlords had converted to Islam and were, largely, repairing the damage.

### Foods of the Middle East

Ibn Battuta described many of the foods grown in Egypt, Damascus and the other places he travelled. It was rare for people to come across foods from foreign lands unless it was somehow dried or preserved. He wrote about carob pods, which taste a bit like chocolate, as well as other typical Middle-Eastern foods such as dates, figs, raisins, different varieties of olives and olive oil, breads and cheeses, cherries and melons.

water tanks on the road between Madinah and Baghdad. For Ibn Battuta and the other thirsty people and animals in the caravan these were a godsend and helped them survive the long journey through the desert. The tanks and the wells that fed them had been built on the orders of Zubayda, the wife of the famous Caliph Harun al-Rashid.

Ibn Battuta took a detour to Basra, which had been famous for its learning before going on to Baghdad. But even this city had not yet recovered from the disasters of the previous century.

*In his own words*

**" I was present once at the Friday prayers in the mosque and when the Imam rose to deliver his sermon he made many terrible mistakes in grammar. In astonishment, I mentioned this to the qadi, who said, 'In this town there is not a man left who knows anything about the subject of grammar.' "**

It was while travelling onwards from Basra that Ibn Battuta decided 'never, so far as possible, to cover a second time any road that I had once travelled'. So rather than taking the direct route to Baghdad, Ibn Battuta diverted east, into Persia. Although the Persians still spoke Persian, Arabic was widely understood and spoken by scholars and the educated classes, so Ibn

A preacher in Basra.

Battuta was able to communicate easily in the social circles that he mixed with.

Travelling by horse and foot, the Moroccan stopped at Isfahan, the orchard city, and Shiraz, the garden city of ancient Persia. Both had been great intellectual centres, and would be again, but since the Mongol invasion both were still shadows of their former selves.

Onwards he went to Baghdad, the erstwhile intellectual, cultural and political capital of the Islamic world, only to find it a skeleton of its former self. Knowing how much had been destroyed might explain the roundabout nature of his approach and when he

### How did Ibn Battuta pay for his travels?

The short answer is that he didn't. In his time, a ruler was supposed to be generous, so Ibn Battuta would present himself at court and be given money, clothes, accommodation, and even slaves. He could do this because he was a scholar and the further he travelled from his homeland the more welcome he became and the more generous the gifts he received. At one point he says in his diaries that he dare not tell the reader how many horses he has acquired in case the reader doesn't believe him.

Coin of Abu Sa'id Bahadur Khan.

finally reached the city Ibn Battuta found it 'for the most part in ruins'.

He found the Sultan Abu Sa'id Bahadur Khan there and Ibn Battuta joined his caravan as the sultan left Baghdad to travel through his realm.

The royal caravan was fast moving, and after a whistle stop tour of the country Ibn Battuta found himself back in Baghdad, from where he joined another caravan returning to Makkah. There he stopped for a long time, at least one year and possibly as long as three.

*"I remained at Makkah all that year, giving myself up entirely to pious exercises and leading a most agreeable existence. After the next Pilgrimage, I spent another year there, and yet another after that."*

Although he does not mention it in the *Rihla*, Ibn Battuta almost certainly also used this time to broaden and deepen his knowledge of Islamic law, attending lectures at the Haram, the main college in Makkah. These studies were to prove invaluable in future. For this sojourn in the holy city was, for Ibn Battuta, like the deep breath a diver takes before jumping into the sea; now his travels were really about to begin.

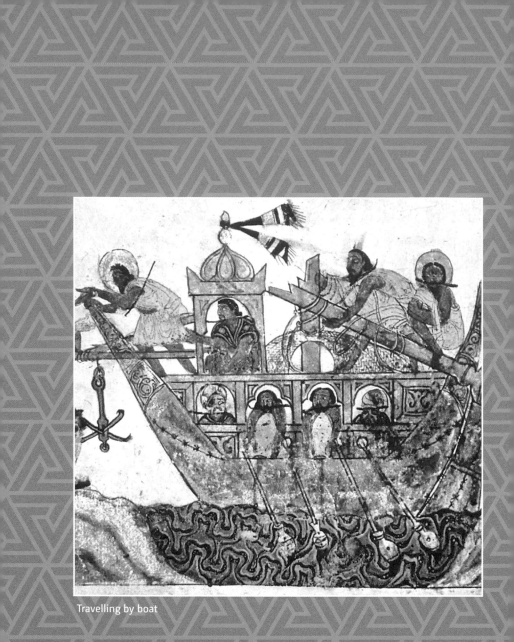
Travelling by boat

## CHAPTER FOUR

# The long road

Ibn Battuta left Makkah for Yemen. The young scholar had
made the pilgrimage; there was now no religious reason for
him to press on. But he did. This departure from Makkah
marked a turn in his adventures: now he was travelling
for the sake of travel, for the new horizons and peoples he
might meet, for the sheer wonder of a world to discover.

Embarking from the port of Aden, Ibn Battuta
travelled down the east coast of Africa. His first stop, at
a port called Zeila, did not impress him, as he found the
place 'the dirtiest, most abominable, and most stinking
town in the world'. However, sailing south, his ship
came first to Mogadishu, whose citizens enjoyed the
fruits of their trade across the Indian Ocean. 'A single
person…eats as much as a whole company of us would
eat…and they are corpulent and fat in the extreme'.
Continuing south, Ibn Battuta crossed the equator. He
was now in the southern hemisphere. Stopping briefly in
Mombasa and Zanzibar, Ibn Battuta's southern progress
finally ended at Kilwa, an island off today's Tanzania.
Here the monsoon winds meant that his ship could only
stay there for a few weeks before heading north again,
eventually making landfall in Zafar in Arabia.

Such was Ibn Battuta's desire to travel that it even

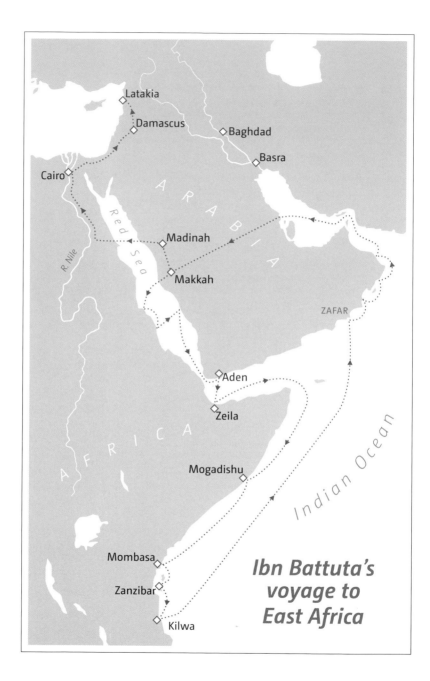

*Ibn Battuta's voyage to East Africa*

overcame his general reluctance to put himself at the mercy of the sea. A true landlubber, Ibn Battuta does not say much about the ships he travelled on, although he does mention one boat he refused to take.

*In his own words*

*❝We embarked here on a boat which they called a jalba. The Sharif Mansur embarked on another and wanted me to go with him, but I refused. He had a number of camels in his jalba and that frightened me, as I had never travelled on sea before. ❞*

But Ibn Battuta couldn't keep travelling without any destination in mind and in the end he decided to go to India. He had heard that the Sultan of Delhi was keen to employ Muslim scholars, and so he hoped to find a job at his court. It was autumn of 1330 and he was 26.

Having decided where to go Ibn Battuta was impatient to leave. However, due to the timetable of the monsoon winds across the Indian Ocean, no boat was available to take him on the direct route to Delhi. So from the port of Latakia in Syria, Ibn Battuta boarded a Genoese – hence Christian-run – boat and set sail for Anatolia, the country that is today called Turkey. Although Ibn Battuta was a devout Muslim, he often encountered Christians in his travels around the Mediterranean and almost always got on well with them.

On board a boat.

41

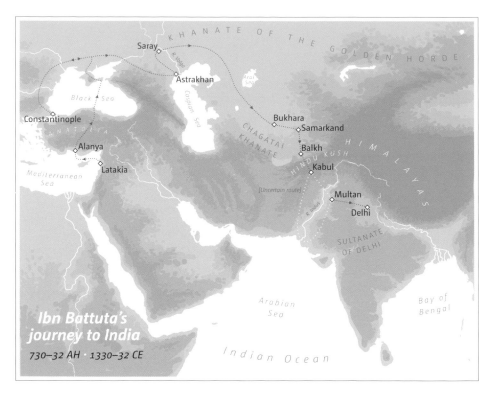

**Ibn Battuta's
journey to India**
*730–32 AH · 1330–32 CE*

*"We were ten nights at sea, and the Christian treated us
kindly and took no passage money from us."*

Arriving at the city of Alanya, Ibn Battuta entered a new
world. The Turks, nomadic peoples from Central Asia,
had migrated westward and were in the long process of
conquering Anatolia when Ibn Battuta arrived in 1330.
Although they were also Muslims, the Turks had some
very different customs from the people Ibn Battuta had
known before. But one of these customs was to prove very
useful to a traveller like Ibn Battuta.

At his next stop in Antalya a rather poorly dressed man asked Ibn Battuta and his travelling companions to come for dinner. Ibn Battuta accepted, but was worried that the man would not be able to afford to feed them all. Unknown to Ibn Battuta the man was the shaykh of the local *fityan* association – a group of young men, usually tailors, cobblers and the like, who banded together in each city to help each other and provide support for travellers – who ensured Ibn Battuta could travel through Anatolia safely and well-fed.

*In his own words*

**"We stayed altogether 14 days with this sultan. Every night he sent us food, fruit, sweetmeats and candles, and gave me in addition a hundred pieces of gold, a thousand dirhams, a complete set of garments and a Greek slave called Michael."**

Another of Ibn Battuta's observations from Anatolia was on the treatment of women in society.

*In his own words*

**"A remarkable thing which I saw in this country was the respect shown to women by the Turks, for they hold a more dignified position than the men. The first time that I saw a princess was when I saw the wife of the amir in her wagon... When she reached the amir he rose before her and greeted her and sat her beside him... I saw also the wives of the merchants and common people... since Turkish women do not veil their faces. Sometimes a woman will be accompanied by her husband and anyone seeing him would think that he was one of her servants."**

Ibn Battuta always had a nose for power and influence, and at the time there was no power in the region of the Black Sea greater than that of Ozbeg, the khan of the Golden Horde.

Ozbeg was a descendant of the Mongol leader, Genghis Khan, and his realm, the Golden Horde, stretched far to the north of the Black Sea. To catch up with him Ibn Battuta took a ship across the Black Sea to the Crimean Peninsula, only to learn that Ozbeg had set off inland on a 700-mile journey to the Volga River. Nothing daunted Ibn Battuta so he hired wagons and oxen and set off in pursuit of Ozbeg. When he caught up with the khan's travelling caravan, it was a sight like no other.

Helmet inscribed with the name of Ozbeg Khan.

*In his own words*

**❝ We saw a vast town on the move with all its inhabitants, containing mosques and bazaars, the smoke from the kitchens rising in the air (for they cook while on the march), and horse-drawn wagons transporting them. ❞**

A Mongol encampment.

Ibn Battuta, who had camped and set his standard up in front of his tent, was spotted by one of the khan's

wives, who sent greetings, which he returned with a present. The khan's wife took the travelling scholar under her protection. Ibn Battuta now had a contact to take him right to Ozbeg himself. Attached to the caravan, and with his own wagon to travel in, Ibn Battuta made the acquaintance of all four of the khan's wives as a preliminary to meeting Ozbeg. As always, Ibn Battuta managed to ingratiate himself with the powerful and, in this case, so much so that he was given leave to go where he would not normally have expected to travel: to the great city of the Byzantine Empire, Constantinople.

One of Ozbeg Khan's wives was called Princess Bayalun, and she was a daughter of Andronicus III, Emperor of Byzantium. When the princess became pregnant, she asked her husband for permission to return to Byzantium to give birth. Ozbeg Khan granted her request, and he also granted Ibn Battuta's request to go with her. This was to be a real journey into new lands, for Byzantium was a Christian land and Ibn Battuta was for the first time venturing outside the **Dar al-Islam**, the House of Islam.

**Wagon wheels**

Mongol and Turkish nomads used wagons to move around the great grass plains of Central Asia as they followed their herds of sheep, cattle and horses. Wagons could have two or four wheels, and were pulled by teams of oxen, camels or horses. To protect occupants from the bitter winds of winter or the searing heat of summer, tents made of felt, called yurts, were set up on the wagons. When the nomads halted, the tents could be taken off the wagons and pitched on the ground. Ibn Battuta tells us that the yurts had little windows, so people riding in the wagons could look out and watch what was going on. A rich nomad could own as many as two hundred wagons.

Oxen.

## Constantinople

Having had the wealth of empire lavished upon it, Constantinople was a city of wonders: the only city in Christendom to match the great cities of the Islamic world. Such was its reputation that it had drawn Vikings down from the far north to seek its treasures, and Ibn Battuta was eager to see the city with his own eyes.

*In his own words*

**"We set out on 10 Shawwal [5 July 1332 or 14 June 1334] in the company of the Princess Bayalun and under her protection. Ozbeg Khan escorted her one stage, then returned, he and the queen and the heir to the throne; the other princesses accompanied her for a second stage and then returned. The Amir Baydara with 5,000 troops travelled with her, and her own troops numbered about 500 horsemen, 200 of whom were her attendant slaves and Greeks, and the remainder Turks. She had with her also about 200 maidens, 400 carts and 2,000 horses, as well as 300 oxen and 200 camels... She left most of her maidens and her baggage at the khan's camp, since she had set out only to pay a visit. "**

Once the procession had reached Greek lands, the princess ceased to practice Islam and returned to her Christian roots. However, she ensured that Ibn Battuta was treated honourably and, when one of the guards laughed at the Muslims for praying, she had him soundly beaten.

About three weeks after setting off, the procession reached 'Constantinople the Great', the capital of Byzantium.

*"The city is enormous in size, and in two parts separated by a great river [the Golden Horn], in which there is a rising and ebbing tide....The part of the city on the eastern bank of the river is called Istambul, and contains the residence of the emperor, the nobles and the rest of the population... The second part, on the western bank of the river, is called Galata, and is reserved to the Frankish Christians who dwell there."*

Constantinople, from the *Nuremberg Chronicle* (1493).

As the guest of Princess Bayalun, Ibn Battuta was given an audience with the Emperor Andronicus III, and a guide was assigned to show him the famous city. Ibn Battuta was most impressed by the great church of Hagia Sophia, but he did not enter it as visitors had first to prostrate themselves in front of a cross before going in.

*"I was out one day with my Greek guide, when we met the former Emperor George who had become a monk. He was walking on foot, wearing haircloth garments and a bonnet of felt, and he had a long white beard and a fine face, which bore traces of his austerities... He took my hand and said, 'I clasp the hand which has entered Jerusalem and the foot which has walked within the Dome of the Rock and the great church of the Holy*

*Sepulchre and Bethlehem,' and he laid his hand upon my feet and passed it over his face. I was astonished at their good opinion of one who, though not of their religion, had entered these places.* **"**

As this testimony indicates, Ibn Battuta was a sympathetic witness to Byzantium despite its long history of conflict

with Islamic foes. It still appeared to him a great, proud and strong city, but in truth it was nearing the end and would eventually fall into Turkic Muslim hands in 1453, 121 years after Ibn Battuta visited.

Although Princess Bayalun did eventually return to her husband, she was in no hurry to leave her

Hagia Sophia.

homeland and Ibn Battuta left Byzantium without her. The journey back to Ozbeg Khan took him into a winter the likes of which he had never known.

*In his own words*

**"***I had to wear three fur coats and two pairs of trousers, one lined. On my feet I had woollen boots, with a pair of linen-lined boots on top of these and a pair of horse skin boots lined with bearskin on top of these again. I performed my ablutions with hot water close to the fire, but every drop of water froze instantly! When I washed my face the water ran down my beard and froze. Water dripping from my nose froze on my moustache. I couldn't mount my horse because of the quantity of clothes I was wearing, and my companions had to help me into the saddle.* **"**

But one of the few advantages to travelling in winter was that the rivers froze, allowing Ibn Battuta and his companions to ride along the snowy highway of the River Volga to Ozbeg Khan's new city of Saray. There he presented his report to the khan.

This was as far north as Ibn Battuta would travel in his journeys and, arriving in the bitter cold of winter, he was probably more than happy at the thought of turning south to India. The road he would take was the most storied highway in history: the Silk Road.

Taking the Silk Road, Ibn Battuta passed the Caspian and Aral seas, stopping at fabled Bukhara and Samarkand, where he met another Mongol ruler, the Chagatai Khan, desecendant of Genghis Khan's second son. But before Ibn Battuta could leave the harsh climes of central Asia for the more hospitable climate of India, he had to head south over the great mountain barrier of the Himalayas, through the Hindu Kush.

*In his own words*

**"On the road there is a mountain called Hindu Kush, which means 'Slayer of Indians', because the slave boys and girls who are brought from India die there in large numbers as a result of the extreme cold and the quantity of snow. We... crossed this mountain by a continuous march from before dawn to sunset. We kept spreading felt cloths in front of the camels for them to tread on so that they should not sink in the snow. "**

Riders crossing a river.

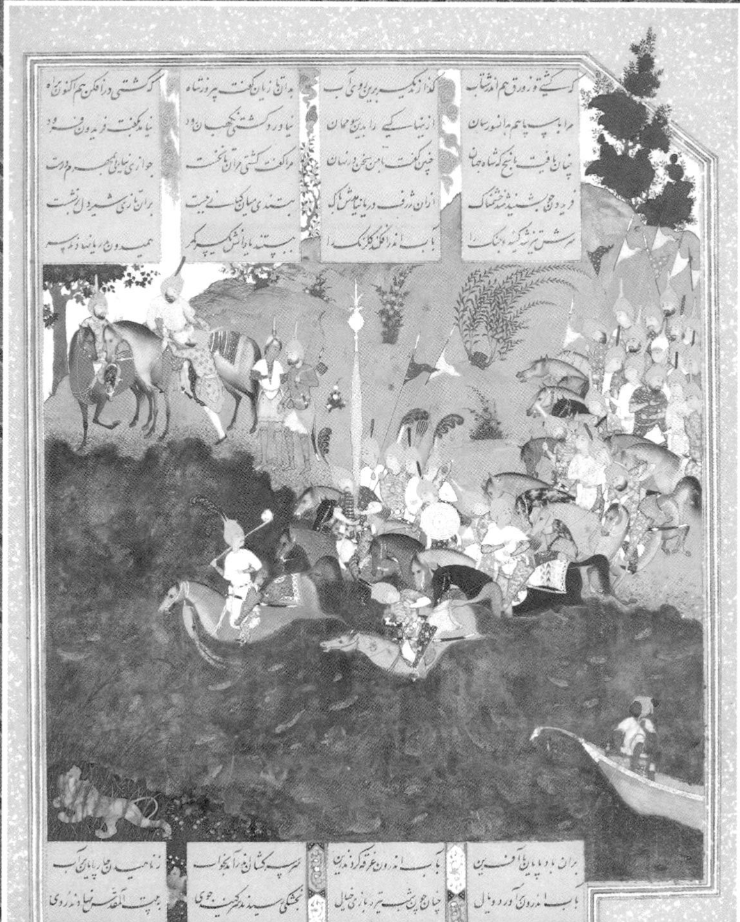

## CHAPTER FIVE

# From riches to rags in India

Ibn Battuta and the caravan he was travelling with reached the Indus River on 12 September 1333. The journey through the territories making up modern-day Afghanistan and Pakistan to get to India had been perilous.

*In his own words*

**" During our passage we had a skirmish with Afghan warriors. They were posted on the lower slope of the hill, but we shot arrows at them and they fled. Our party was travelling light and had about four thousand horses. I had camels, as a result of which I became separated from the caravan… From here we entered the great desert which extends for fifteen days and can be traversed only in one season of the year… In this desert blows the deadly samúm wind. "**

On their crossing of the Indus River Ibn Battuta and his caravan were met by officials of the Sultan of Delhi. These men, who acted as spies and customs officers, took the details of everyone in the caravan and their business, and sent word to Delhi.

*In his own words*

**" From Sindh to the city of Delhi, the sultan's capital, it is 50 days' march, but when the intelligence officers write**

***to the sultan from Sind the letter reaches him in five days by the postal service... "***

Standing in India, on the banks of the Indus, Ibn Battuta had reached the furthest frontier of the Islamic world at 29 years old. Nevertheless he would spend 12 years in the sub continent, the longest period in one place during his adventures.

Ibn Battuta was just one of the men who came east to seek service and employment with Sultan Muhammad Tughluq, the ruler of this vast new frontier, who was known far and wide for his generosity. Yet, like most of them, he came to regret this decision, but only after the most extraordinary few years of his extraordinary life.

" *This king is of all men the fondest of making gifts and of shedding blood. His gate is never without some poor man enriched or some living man executed, and stories are current among the people of his generosity and courage and of his cruelty and violence towards criminals. For all that, he is of all men the most humble and the readiest to show equity and justice. The ceremonies of religion are strictly complied with at his court, and he is severe in the matter of attendance at prayer and in punishing those who neglect it.* "

**India**

In the late thirteenth and early fourteenth centuries, the kings of Delhi set out to conquer the rest of India and all but succeeded. By 1333, Muhammad Tughluq was the ruler of most of that huge and diverse country. But Muslims still formed a small proportion of the population, although there were a growing number of converts from the native Hindu population. However, the rulers did not entirely trust these new Muslims and there were considerable tensions between the Indian Muslims and those who could trace their ancestry back to Islamic countries. So the sultans of Delhi sent out word throughout the Islamic world, calling scholars and *qadis*, historians and poets, craftsmen and merchants to this relatively new but vastly wealthy Muslim court.

Muhammad Tughluq was one of the strangest men to ever be king. He was a military genius, and in the first decade of his reign he doubled the size of his realm, bringing most of south India under his control. He was a religious scholar, a poet and a master calligrapher. He learned Arabic and was the patron of scholars and Sufis. But he was also extraordinarily cruel and capricious. When the citizens of Delhi displeased him, he decided to move the capital 400 miles south and, finding a blind man and a cripple left behind, he ordered that the cripple be flung from a catapult and the blind man dragged all the way to the new

Ruins in the
Tughluq capital.

city. Ibn Battuta says that 'he fell to pieces on the road and all of him that reached Dawlat Abad was his leg.'

This was the man with whom Ibn Battuta sought employment, and in fact it all started out very profitably. When Ibn Battuta arrived, the king's court had been moved south to the Deccan plateau in central India. Despite this there were still many important people in Delhi including the sultan's vizier and his blind mother. Ibn Battuta met the vizier in the Hall of a Thousand Pillars, who gave him a gift of 2,000 silver dinars and a comfortable house for his use. But Ibn Battuta knew well that the key meeting would be when he met the sultan himself, and for this he made careful preparations.

Ibn Battuta had made the journey to India intending to gain a post from the famous Muhammad Tughluq and the first impression he made on the sultan would be vital – for if he failed to impress, then there would be no second chance. Gift giving was key to making the right impression, and Ibn Battuta was expected to make a present to the sultan on meeting him. However, Muhammad Tughluq was known for returning any first-time gift many times over, and local merchants relied upon this to make a swift profit. One of these merchants struck a deal with Ibn Battuta, advancing him a considerable loan, as well as camels and presents, on the understanding that when the sultan returned and exceeded the gift, the merchant would take a big chunk of the profits.

Word came that the sultan was camped 10 kilometres [seven miles] from the city. It must have been with some nervousness that Ibn Battuta went out to meet Muhammad Tughluq, taking his carefully prepared gifts with him but, more importantly, the skills he had honed at making a good impression on the powerful and the rich.

Coins of Muhammad Tughluq.

*In his own words*

**"** *I approached the sultan, who took my hand and shook it, and continuing to hold it addressed me most affably in Persian, saying, 'Your arrival is blessed; be at ease, I shall be compassionate to you and give you such favours that your fellow-countrymen will hear of it and come to join you.' Then he asked me where I came from and I answered him, and every time he said any encouraging word to me I kissed his hand, until I had kissed it seven times.* **"**

Having found favour with the sultan, Ibn Battuta joined his return into Delhi. As further evidence of his

generosity, Muhammad Tughluq ordered that small catapults on the backs of the elephants should fire parcels of gold and silver coins into the watching crowds. And as evidence of the favour he had found with the sultan, Ibn Battuta was appointed *qadi* of Delhi and allocated the income of two villages – 12,000 silver dinars a year. The average family lived on five dinars a month.

Ibn Battuta had suddenly become a very rich man.

As a *qadi*, Ibn Battuta had to hear all sorts of cases. When the harvest failed, people started searching for scapegoats for their misfortune and one of these unfortunates was brought before him.

Qutub Minaret,
Delhi.

*In his own words*

**" During the famine in Delhi they brought [someone they claimed was] a witch to me, saying that she had eaten the heart of a boy. I ordered them to take her to the sultan's lieutenant. He commanded that she should be put to the test. They filled four jars with water, tied them to her hands and feet and threw her into the River Jumna. She did not sink, and by this she was known to**

*be a witch; if she had not floated she would not have been one. Then he ordered her to be burned in the fire. Her ashes were collected by the men and women of the town, for they believe that anyone who fumigates himself with them is safe against a witch's sorcery during that year.* **"**

But the favours the sultan had lavished on Ibn Battuta could also be taken away, particularly if the sultan heard that he was visiting men he considered enemies. Such a man was the Sufi shaykh, Shihab al-Din. Like many Sufis, Shihab al-Din tried to keep away from politics. But Muhammad Tughluq was not the sort of man to take no for an answer and insisted that the shaykh attend his court. When Shihab al-Din first refused to do what the sultan ordered, Muhammad Tughluq had his beard plucked out hair by hair. When he next refused an order to appear at court, the sultan had him arrested, tortured and beheaded. Unfortunately, Ibn Battuta had been one of Shihab al-Din's visitors.

After the execution of Shihab al-Din, Muhammad Tughluq asked for a list of everyone who had visited the shaykh. One of the names on the list was Ibn Battuta. He was imprisoned, with little hope of escape – seemingly at the end of his journey.

*In his own words*

**"** *The sultan had thoughts of punishing me and gave orders that four of his slaves should remain constantly beside me in the audience hall. When this action is taken with anyone, it rarely happens that he escapes. I fasted* *for five days on end, reading the Qur'an from cover to cover each day, and tasting nothing but water. After five days I broke my fast and then continued to fast for another four days on end, and was set free after the shaykh's death, praise be to God.* **"**

Food being given to a captive.

He had survived the suspicions of the sultan and learned how dangerous being friends with him could be. Thoroughly terrified, he wanted to leave, but would Muhammad Tughluq let him go?

In the end, the only excuse he could think of was to request permission to make the pilgrimage to Makkah. The sultan agreed but then, just as Ibn Battuta was getting ready to start heading back west, Muhammad Tughluq called for him again. 'I have sent for you to act as my ambassador to the emperor of China, for I know of your love of travel.' What else could Ibn Battuta do but accept?

With Ibn Battuta in charge, the mission left Delhi on 2 August 1341. Ibn Battuta was now 37, he had been away from home for 16 years and he was about to travel to the eastern end of the known world.

At this time it was the custom for rulers to send lavish

gifts with their ambassadors. The ruler of China – another descendant of Genghis Khan – had sent 100 slaves, 500 rolls of velvet and silk, perfume, clothes covered with jewels and beautiful weapons as his present to the sultan. But Muhammad Tughluq was not to be outdone.

*In his own words*

**"** *A hundred thoroughbred horses, a hundred white slaves, a hundred Hindu dancing- and singing-girls, 1,200 rolls of cloth, gold and silver candelabra and basins, brocade robes, caps, quivers, swords, gloves embroidered with pearls, and 15 eunuchs.* **"**

Ibn Battuta was leading as much treasure trove as diplomatic mission. As such, it needed serious protection. So the sultan sent a thousand horsemen to accompany Ibn Battuta and the returning delegation of Chinese ambassadors. The plan was to head south through India and then catch a boat to China. But the mission turned into a disaster. Perhaps that should not have come as too much of a surprise. As a judge and scholar, Ibn Battuta had many accomplishments, but the skills to lead a semi-military diplomatic expedition through the troubled provinces of India and on to China were not among them.

Not far south of Delhi, the embassy was attacked by rebels and, though the attackers were driven off, Ibn Battuta got separated from the soldiers and was captured and stripped of everything he possessed. The rest of the surviving rebels went off in search of more plunder, but Ibn Battuta was left with three men who

A man at a well.

were given orders to kill him. These three couldn't seem to make up their minds what to do however, and when a small group of the bandits returned, Ibn Battuta was set free. But he was alone, without food, water or weapons, in a land that was full of rebels. For seven days he wandered, keeping clear of villages and scavenging what food and water he found. By the eighth day he was desperate and stood naked apart from his trousers, for even his shirt had been stolen from him.

Coming to a well, Ibn Battuta lowered his shoe into the hole to draw up water. The rope came undone, and he lost his shoe at the bottom of the well. Still parched, Ibn Battuta tied his other shoe to the rope and lowered it into the well. This time the knot stayed tight, and he drew the rope up with his shoe bucket on the end, and drank what must have been quite flavoursome water. Still thirsty, he repeated this until he was satisfied, whereupon he realised that he only had one shoe and many miles still to go.

So it was a huge relief when a man approached and offered him first the Arabic greeting, '**As-salamu 'alaykum**', and then asked him in Persian who he was.

Ibn Battuta answered in Persian that he was 'a man astray' to which the stranger replied, 'As am I.' After giving Ibn Battuta something to eat and drink, the stranger asked again for Ibn Battuta's name, to which he replied, 'Muhammad.' When Ibn Battuta asked the man's name, the stranger replied, 'Blithe Heart.' So weak had the Moroccan become, Ibn Battuta lost consciousness and the stranger had to carry him on his back to the nearest village. When Ibn Battuta woke he was in a friendly village. Of 'Blithe Heart' there was no sign.

**" I thought of the man who had carried me on his shoulders and I remembered what Shaykh al-Murshidi had told me... 'My brother, Dilshad, will deliver you from a misfortune which will befall you there.' I remembered too how he had said, when I asked him his name, 'Blithe Heart,' which, translated into Persian, is Dilshad. "**

A messenger was sent out from the village and soon companions from his embassy came to claim Ibn Battuta. They were astonished that he was still alive. No doubt thanking God that he did not have to report back to the sultan that the mission had failed, Ibn Battuta rejoined the caravan and it continued on its journey south.

Disaster struck again when they came to the port of Calicut in south India. Since there were so many people, animals and goods travelling to China, Ibn Battuta decided to hire two Chinese junks for the voyage. He was going to travel on the larger one, but since he could not have a cabin to himself on it, decided to transfer all his belongings and slaves to the smaller ship. Since the loading took place on a Thursday, Ibn Battuta decided to stay ashore so that he could take part in the Friday prayers and then embark. But a storm blew up and the ship carrying the presents for the emperor of China sank, while the smaller vessel carrying all Ibn Battuta's belongings was blown out to sea and out of sight.

A Chinese ship of the Yuan Dynasty.

The mission was a complete failure. The treasure was either at the bottom of the sea or looted by beach scavengers. The slaves and servants destined for the emperor of China had all drowned.

*In his own words*

**"** *I was alone on the beach with but one slave whom I had enfranchised. When he saw what had befallen me he deserted me, and I had nothing left with me at all except ten dinars and the carpet I had slept on... I intended at first to return to the sultan to tell him what had happened to the present, but afterwards I was afraid that he would find fault with what I had done and ask me why I had not stayed with the present.* **"**

What was he to do? Initially, he sought employment
with Jamal al-Din, the Sultan of Honavar, one of the
small maritime kingdoms on the south-west coast of
India. Jamal al-Din put Ibn Battuta to work – by prayer.
For three months, Ibn Battuta recited the Qur'an daily
on the sultan's behalf. But this was work that, while
it might bring spiritual benefit, brought little in the
way of monetary reward, for the sultan had quartered
him in a small house and not even given him any
servants. Determined to gain a position more fitting
to his status, Ibn Battuta volunteered to take part in a
raid on a nearby sultanate. Despite his lack of military
experience, the expedition of 52 ships, which set sail

on 12 October 1342, proved a great success, with Ibn Battuta acquitting himself bravely.

**"** *The inhabitants were prepared for battle and had set up mangonels, which they discharged against the vessels when they advanced in the morning. Those on the ships jumped into the water, shields and swords in hand, and I jumped with them, and God granted victory to the Muslims. We entered the city at the point of the sword and the greater part of the infidels fled into their sultan's palace, but when we threw fire into it they came out and we seized them ...* **"**

But Jamal al-Din's small sultanate in turn fell prey to an attack. Ibn Battuta, seeing no good reason to stick around, managed to slip through the forces beseiging the sultan and make his get away.

Unable to go back, Ibn Battuta decided to go on, to continue with his travels and to carry on towards China. In 1343, he took ship from Calicut and landed in the Maldive Islands.

The Mosque in Quanzhou, China.

## CHAPTER SIX
# An ambassador to the East

The inhabitants of the Maldives, a group of more than a thousand coral islands, only embraced Islam in the early 12th century. When Ibn Battuta landed he was worried that if word got out that a *qadi* from the court of the Sultan of Delhi had arrived, they would not let him leave. As a precaution he asked his companions not to tell the vizier who he was. But the crew of another ship recognised him and, sure enough, as a legal scholar who had studied in Makkah itself, Ibn Battuta found himself made *qadi* of the Maldive Islands.

A queen was the ostensible ruler of the Maldives, but the real power lay in the hands of her husband, the vizier, who wanted this illustrious foreign *qadi* to strengthen his rule.

*In his own words*

**" Most of the women in the Maldive Islands wear only an apron from their waists to the ground, while the rest of their bodies are uncovered. When I was the qadi there, I tried to put an end to this practice and ordered them to wear clothes, but I was not successful. I did not allow any woman to come into my presence during a lawsuit unless her body was covered, but apart from that I was completely unable to change their minds. "**

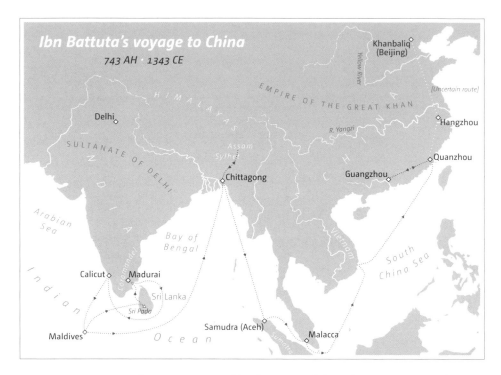

Ibn Battuta's voyage to China
743 AH · 1343 CE

Ibn Battuta quickly discovered that there are worse things than being forced to remain on a tropical island paradise, and he soon made himself even more at home marrying several times. Unfortunately, these marriages to well-connected local women embroiled him in the politics of the islands. He may even have become part of a plot to oust the queen and her vizier.

*In his own words*

**"** *I made a pact with two of the ministers that I should go to the land of Coromandel, the king of which was the husband of my wife's sister, and fetch troops from there to bring the islands under his authority, and that I should* *be his representative in them. I arranged that the signal between us should be the hoisting of white flags on the ships; when they saw these they were to rise in revolt on the shore.* **"**

However, the plan failed and in the end Ibn Battuta sailed to Sri Lanka. Ever the traveller, he made the arduous trip into the rugged hills of the country's interior in order to climb a mountain: Sri Pada or Adam's Peak. His appetite to climb it may have been whetted by his sighting of the mountain from far out to sea 'rising up into the sky like a column of smoke'.

### Sri Pada or 'Adam's Peak'

Sri Pada is the fifth highest mountain in Sri Lanka, rising to 2,243 metres [7,359 feet]. At the summit there is an indentation in the shape of a huge footprint. Buddhists believe that the footprint was made by the lord Buddha. For Hindus, the footprint is that of the god Shiva. Some Muslims and Christians there both claim that it is the footprint of Adam.

*" When we climbed it [Adam's Peak] we saw the clouds below us, shutting out the views of its base… [before the peak] the pilgrims leave their belongings and ascend the two miles to the summit of the mountain where the Foot is… It is eleven spans long. "*

Ibn Battuta spent three days camping at the summit of Adam's Peak before returning to the coast and boarding a boat to continue his journey. However, his ship was soon wrecked on the coast of India during a storm. Villagers rescued the sailors and passengers and sent word to the local ruler, Sultan Ghiyath al-Din, who sent for Ibn Battuta and greeted him warmly. For a while it seemed possible that Ibn Battuta might find a position at his court in Ma'bar, in the south east of India, but Ibn Battuta quickly realised he had no wish to stay. For as he travelled with the sultan and his soldiers through his realm, Ibn Battuta saw first hand how they treated the local Hindu population.

The tomb of Ghiyath al-Din, Delhi.

*" All the idol-worshippers they found in the jungle were taken prisoner and brought to the camp with their wives and children. In the morning the idol-worshippers that our troops had captured the previous day were divided into four groups and impaled at the four gates of the camp. Their women and little children were also slaughtered with knives and the women were tied by their hair to poles. That is a terrible, dastardly deed which I have never known any king to do. That was why God brought him to a speedy end. "*

So it was hardly surprising that Ibn Battuta decided to leave as soon as possible, but because of the season and the winds, he ended up sailing back and forth along the coast, and even returning briefly to the Maldives, before he found a boat that would take him further east.

China was still his ultimate destination. A land of wealth and culture that proved irresistible to Ibn Battuta.

Being Ibn Battuta, however, he made the most of his journey east, stopping along the way at Chittagong in modern-day Bangladesh before taking passage on one of the ocean-going Chinese junks east, to Sumatra, arriving in 1345. The sultan there was the easternmost Muslim ruler in the world at the time. To carry on would be to venture beyond the *Dar al-Islam*, the lands where Islam held sway.

He did. The Silk Road had an ocean route as well as a land route, and this is what he was now following, up the Malaysian peninsula, with stops along the way at Malacca

The Mosque at Guangzhou (Canton).

and then in Vietnam. Setting sail from Vietnam, Ibn
Battuta arrived in Quanzhou in south-eastern China.
He had made it.

In China, Ibn Battuta made contact with resident
Muslims, travelling to Guangzhou, Hangzhou and,
eventually, Beijing, where he presented himself at the
Imperial court as the long-expected ambassador from
Muhammad Tughluq, Sultan of Delhi.

*In his own words*

**" The land of China is of vast extent, and abounding in
produce, fruits, grain, gold and silver. In this respect there
is no country in the world that can rival it ... The Chinese
are of all peoples the most skilful in the arts and possessed
of the greatest mastery of them ... China is the safest and
best regulated of countries for a traveller. A man may go
by himself on a nine months' journey, carrying with him
large sums of money, without any fear on that account. "**

However, this most intrepid of travellers found China a shock. Normally Ibn Battuta would make a point of seeing all the local sights and visiting any important persons in the town where he was staying. But China was simply too different for him to enjoy; strange though it might seem for a man who had travelled so widely and seen so much, in China Ibn Battuta seems to have suffered a severe case of culture shock.

The Great Wall of China – which Ibn Battuta refers to in the *Rihla* – here a section dating from the Han Dynasty, already over a thouand years old in Ibn Battuta's time.

*In his own words*

**" The land of China, in spite of all that is agreeable in it, did not attract me. On the contrary, I was very saddened that paganism had such a strong hold over it. Whenever I went out of my house I used to see so many revolting things, and that distressed me so much that I used to stay indoors and only go out if I really needed to. "**

For the first time an unhappy traveller, Ibn Battuta set sail from China in 1346. Although he may not have intended to at the time, he was heading home.

Damascus: the Dome of the Treasury at the Umayyad Mosque.

## CHAPTER SEVEN

# The final journey

In 1348, having sailed across the Indian Ocean and crossing through Persia, Ibn Battuta arrived back in Damascus. He had first visited the city in 1326, twelve years before. Ibn Battuta was returning to the places and people he had left behind on his travels and not least among these were wives and children. In Damascus he hastened to learn what had happened to one of them.

*In his own words*

❝ *I had left a wife of mine there pregnant, and I learned while I was in India that she had borne a male child. When I received the news, I sent 40 gold dinars to the boy's maternal grandfather to pay for his cure and education. When I arrived in Damascus my only thought was to enquire after my son. I went to the mosque, where I made myself known to the imam and asked him about the boy. He replied, 'He has been dead for these past 12 years* [that is, he died soon after he was born].' *He told me that a scholar from Tangier was living nearby, so I went to see him to ask about my father's relatives. He told me that my father had died 15 years ago, but that my mother was still alive.* ❞

These early tidings of death were a prophecy of what was to come. For as Ibn Battuta rode home, the Black

A sick woman with her attendants.

Death rode alongside him. The disease had started on the plains of Central Asia, where Ibn Battuta had journeyed many years before, and it spread with the caravans, east, west and south. By the time it had run its course, the plague would have killed about a third of the population of Asia, the Middle East and Europe, altering forever countries and peoples. But Ibn Battuta was a witness to its first, devastating impact upon Damascus and some of the other great cities of the Islamic world.

*In his own words*

**" Early in June we heard at Aleppo that the plague had broken out at Gaza, and that the number of deaths there reached over a thousand a day. On travelling to Hims I found that the plague had broken out there: about 300 people died of it on the day that I arrived. So I went on to Damascus. The number of deaths among them reached a maximum of 2,400 a day. Thereafter I journeyed to 'Ajalun and thence to Jerusalem, where I found that the ravages of the plague had ceased. We revisited Hebron, and thence went to Gaza, the greater part of which we found deserted because of the number who died there of the plague. We continued on to Alexandria. Here we found the plague was diminishing in intensity, though the number of deaths had previously reached 1,080 a day. I then travelled to Cairo, where I was told that the number of deaths during the epidemic rose to 21,000**

*a day... Finally we reached the town of Taza, where I learned the news of my mother's death of the plague – may God Most High have mercy on her. "*

Although he had known of his father's death since arriving in Damascus, Ibn Battuta had hoped to return home to see his mother. But the plague that had dogged his return had gone on ahead of him, and claimed her before she could see the son who had been away for so long.

## The last journey

Ibn Battuta returned home to find his parents both dead. It was 1349. He had been away for twenty-four years. The young man who had left on the pilgrimage to Makkah was long gone. The man who returned was 45. He had travelled further than anyone else of his time, seen things and met people across a vast expanse of the world; he had been raised to riches and feared for his life; he had been shipwrecked many times, attacked by bandits and armies, abandoned and found again. But now Ibn Battuta was home.

Rats helped spread the black plague by carrying infected fleas.

Naturally, he did not stay long.

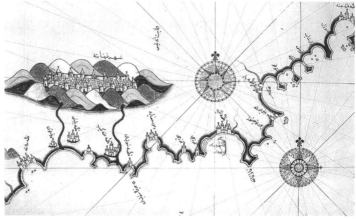

A map showing Granada.

Instead, he set off for the land that was closest to Morocco: Spain. Just across the Straits of Gibraltar, much of Spain had been under Muslim rule for centuries. It was to Granada that Ibn Battuta travelled, finding it as beautiful then as visitors do today. He also met a young literary scholar and kept him entranced with his tales of travel and far away places. That scholar was Ibn Juzayy and five years later he would get the chance to write down Ibn Battuta's reminiscences, turning them into the *Rihla* that has come down to us.

But Spain was not the end of Ibn Battuta's travellings. There was one final part of the Muslim world that he had not visited. Although they lay not far to the south of his home country the Muslim kingdoms of central Africa were separated from Morocco by the vast desert of the Sahara. However, undaunted, early in 1352 Ibn Battuta joined a caravan and set off south for the desert kingdom of Mali. Tuareg nomads, clad in their sky-blue robes, still make this journey today and reckon on it taking 63 days. Ibn

Battuta does not tell us how long he took, merely noting that the journey was long and arduous. But at least he survived it. Many did not.

After passing the winter in the last town north of the desert proper, Ibn Battuta set out with a caravan to cross the most dangerous section of the Sahara. They were fortunate, for some rain had fallen in the days before and their animals were able to drink from pools left by the rain. But the desert remained hazardous, and one of Ibn Battuta's party got lost and was never found. Ibn Battuta tells us of the fate of another unfortunate traveller.

## Mali

The West African empire of Mali was famous throughout the Islamic world for its wealth. This wealth was based upon the gold dug from its mines. So productive were these mines that scholars believe two thirds of the world's gold supply came from them at this time. But the Sahara Desert produced little else apart from gold, so the long caravans carried gold to the cities of Africa and the Middle East, and returned with all the fruits of civilisation. Other caravans headed south from Mali, into the grasslands and jungles of Central Africa, and returned with ivory, animal hides and slaves.

Mali on a medieval map featuring Mansa Musa, a notorious king.

*In his own words*

❝ *We passed a caravan on the way and they told us that some of their party had become separated from them. We found one of them dead under a shrub with his clothes on and a whip in his hand. The water was only about a mile away from him.* ❞

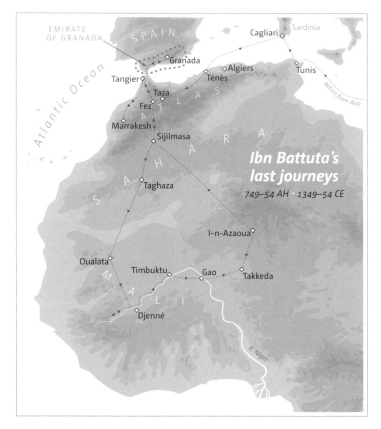

**Ibn Battuta's last journeys**
749–54 AH · 1349–54 CE

But eventually he arrived in the kingdom of Mali. There he discovered that these Muslims were different in some ways from Muslims of other lands.

*In his own words*

**"** *Their women are shown more respect than the men. The state of affairs among these people is indeed extraordinary. Their men show no signs of jealousy whatever; no one claims descent from his father, but on the contrary from his mother's brother. A man's heirs are his sister's sons, not his own sons. This is a thing*

*I have seen nowhere else in the world except among the Indians of Malabar. But those people are heathens, whereas these are Muslims, punctilious in observing the hours of prayer, studying books of law and memorizing the Qur'an. Yet their women show no bashfulness before men and do not veil themselves, though they are assiduous in attending the prayers.* **"**

And if Ibn Battuta found the conduct of the women surprising, he found Sultan Sulayman, the ruler of Mali, even stranger. After he had seen the sultan in audience, Ibn Battuta was told to expect the sultan's gift. Bearing in mind that the kingdom of Mali was legendary for its wealth, and that Ibn Battuta had been showered with gifts by kings and sultans around the world, what happened next came as something of a surprise.

*In his own words*

**"***I got up, thinking that it would be robes of honour and money, but behold! It was three loaves of bread and a piece of beef fried in butter and a gourd containing a yoghurt. When I saw this I burst out laughing.* **"**

On 27 February 1353 (22 Muharram 754), Ibn Battuta left Sulayman's court and nearly a year later he reached Fez, the capital of Morocco. Sultan Abu 'Inan had commanded his return, and he must have listened with great interest to Ibn Battuta's stories of the world. For it was this sultan who asked Ibn Battuta to tell the tale of his voyages to a young writer attached to his court, and it was this writer, Ibn Juzayy, who turned Ibn Battuta's memories into the *Rihla* we have today.

The tale of his travels told to Ibn Juzayy and written out with the title *A Gift to Those Who Contemplate the Wonders of Cities and the Marvels of Travelling* (although it is invariably known as the *Rihla*, 'Journey'), the great traveller settled, so far as we know, into retirement. Ever the judge, Ibn Battuta was appointed a *qadi* in Morocco and rendered his judgements, leavened by an experience broader than any other man living, until he set out on his final journey, the journey from which no man returns, in 1368 or 69.

The place said to be the tomb of Ibn Battuta, in Tangier.

At the end of the *Rihla*, its scribe, Ibn Juzayy, adds these words of his own:

Here ends the narrative which I have abridged from the dictation of Shaykh Abu Abdallah Muhammad ibn Battuta (may God ennoble him). It is plain to any man of intelligence that this shaykh is the traveller of the age: and if one were to say the traveller par excellence of our Muslim community he would be guilty of no exaggeration.

Statue and relief commemorating Ibn Battuta in Quanzhou, China.

## CHAPTER EIGHT

# Epilogue

It's unlikely that any human being before the advent of
modern travel travelled as far or as widely as Ibn Battuta.
So why did he do it? What propelled him onwards, to go
as far from his home as he possibly could?

Our only source on this is the man himself, and what he
tells us in his *Rihla*. But from that, it is clear that the greatest
motive for his journeys was simply the desire to travel: to
see over the next ridge, to look round the next headland and
to meet new people. Ibn Battuta wasn't interested in boldly
going where no man had gone before, nor in seeking out
new civilisations. He was a traveller, not an explorer.

What made his incredible journey possible was the
spread of Islamic culture in a wide, continuous belt from
Spain and north Africa, through the Middle East, to central
and south Asia. Within this culture, there was always a place
for an experienced judge, particularly one with the sort
of credentials that Ibn Battuta had carefully accrued. And
in the further-flung reaches of the *Dar al-Islam* (House of
Islam), it added to the glory of a ruler to have, at his court, a
*qadi* who had studied in Makkah itself. Especially at a time
when they were in short supply in the Islamic world, which
was slowly recovering from the devastation of libraries and
centres of learning during the Mongol incursion.

As to the man himself, he was courteous and correct; in his appearance and demeanour he represented the Muslim ideal of manners. Indeed, it was Ibn Battuta's grace that first opened the door to so many different royal courts around the world, and then kept the gifts flowing from kings who were keen on being seen as benefactors of Muslim scholars.

Ibn Battuta told the stories of his travels to his scribe, Ibn Juzayy, from memory – whatever notes he made were

Two men in discussion.

lost during one of his shipwrecks or skirmishes. Although there are some errors, they are few: Ibn Battuta had a memory that would seem extraordinary today. But as a scholar, he had been trained to memorise information; in a time when books were rare, expensive and not very portable, a scholar had to keep his knowledge in his head.

A token of Ibn Battuta's memory is the number of people he names in the *Rihla*: some 2,000 individuals, from sultans through Sufi shaykhs to ordinary men (in accordance with the custom of the time, few women are named in the *Rihla*). This shows another side to Ibn Battuta: he was an inveterate name dropper, thoroughly enjoying the glory that came from knowing so many of the important men of his time. However, this wish to be among the men who counted was counterbalanced by Ibn Battuta's seeking out of saints and holy men, most of whom avoided the intrigues of court as much as possible.

In fact, attachment and freedom clashed in Ibn Battuta

at many different levels. During his journeys he married often, to as many as ten wives, fathering an unknown number of children. But the call of new horizons always won out over the ties of wife and children. As often as he married, he divorced, leaving his children to be brought up by the family of the wife he had left behind.

Although he travelled so widely, Ibn Battuta was most comfortable within the milieu of educated Muslim scholars, who formed a transnational class, united by knowledge of Arabic and grounded in Islamic jurisprudence. When he travelled beyond the bounds of the Islamic world to China, Ibn Battuta became deeply uncomfortable and, for the first time, he lost his normal profound curiosity, shutting himself away from new sights and experiences. In fact, Ibn Battuta's account of his visit to China is so sketchy that some scholars doubt that he actually went that far, but added it to the *Rihla* to include a trip to the fabled, far-flung land. After all, the Prophet himself had said, "Seek knowledge, even if it be in China."

When Ibn Battuta returned to Morocco in 1353 his travel lust seems finally to have been sated and he settled down as *qadi* of a town there. He probably married again, but this time he remained with his wife and children until, in 1368 or 1369, he made the final journey. Where he died and was buried is unknown.

# Timeline

**24 February 1304** – Ibn Battuta is born in Tangier, Morocco.

**1325** – Ibn Battuta leaves Morocco to perform hajj, the pilgrimage to Makkah.

**Spring 1326** – Ibn Battuta arrives in the port city of Alexandria and visits Cairo, the capital of the Mamluks.

**9 August 1326** – Travels to Damascus via Bethlehem and Jerusalem, and there joins a caravan heading south to Madinah.

**Autumn 1326** –Ibn Battuta spends four days in Madinah then continues to Makkah to complete the hajj.

**17 November 1326** – Ibn Battuta leaves Makkah for Iraq.

**January to July 1327** – Ibn Battuta heads east to Wasit, then on to Basra. He then travels on to Persia, visiting Isfahan and Shiraz.

**18 September 1327** – Joins a caravan leaving Baghdad for Makkah.

**Autumn 1327** – Ibn Battuta spends about a year in Makkah, studying, praying and recuperating from his previous voyages.

**1328** – Embarks on a series of boats, heading south down the Red Sea.

**1329** – Arrives in Aden and sails south down the east coast of Africa, before sailing north to Zafar.

**1330** – Returns to Makkah.

**End 1330** – Heads up the Red Sea to Cairo, then to the port of Latakia, where he takes ship to Alanya in modern-day Turkey.

**1331** – Ibn Battuta travels through Anatolia (modern-day Turkey), then sails across the Black Sea and eventually joins the travelling court of Ozbeg Khan.

**1332** – Visits Constantinople with a caravan taking Princess Bayalun, Ozbeg Khan's wife, for the birth of her first child.

**Autumn/Winter 1332/1333** – Leaves Constantinople. Travels to Astrakhan and on to Saray.

**Spring 1333** –Travels south and east, heading towards India, passing through Bukhara and Samarkand on the way.

**12 September 1333** – Ibn Battuta reaches the River Indus, the traditional frontier of India.

**Late 1334** – Ibn Battuta travels to Delhi to seek a position at the court of the sultan, Muhammad Tughluq.

**8 June 1335** – Ibn Battuta meets Muhammad Tughluq for the first time, gaining a position in the imperial court.

**1341** – Ibn Battuta agrees to lead an embassy to China on behalf of Muhammad Tughluq.

**February 1342** – Disaster strikes the embassy when the ships to carry it to China are sunk in a storm in Calicut.

**April 1342** – Travels to Honavar.

**1343** – Sets sail toward China, but stops in the Maldives on the way.

**Late 1343/1344** – Visits Sri Lanka.

**May 1345** – Sails from the Maldives around the tip of India to Bengal.

**1345** – Takes ship from Chittagong to Samudra in Sumatra.

**April 1346** – Sails to China.

**Autumn 1346** – Leaves China to go home.

**December 1346** – Makes port in Quilon, southern India.

**Early 1348** – Stops briefly in Damascus.

**16 November 1348** – Arrives in Makkah.

**8 November 1349** – Arrives in Fez.

**April 1350** – Travels across the strait of Gibraltar and visits Granada.

**Late 1350** – Ibn Battuta returns to Morocco.

**Autumn 1351** – Leaves Fez to cross the Atlas Mountains.

**February 1352** – Joins a caravan crossing the Sahara Desert to Mali.

**27 February 1353** – Leaves Mali

**1354** – After visiting Timbuktu on his journey back from Mali, Ibn Battuta returns to Morocco, for good.

**1355** – Ibn Battuta tells the story of his travels to Ibn Juzayy, who writes them down as the *Rihla*.

**1368/1369** – Ibn Battuta makes his final journey.

# Glossary

| | |
|---|---|
| **'alim** | a scholar of Islamic law |
| **As-salamu 'alaykum** | the Muslim greeting: peace be upon you |
| **Dar al-Islam** | that part of the world where Islam is the ruling faith |
| **faqih** | a lawyer in Islamic jurisprudence |
| **fityan** | an association of young tradesmen who supported each other and travellers |
| **hadith** | the sayings and actions of the Prophet Muhammad |
| **hajji** | a Muslim who has completed the pilgrimage to Makkah |
| **ijazah** | a certificate, issued by a respected religious scholar or teacher, to teach a book or subject |
| **qadi** | a judge of Islamic law |
| **shaykh** | a Sufi teacher and spiritual leader |
| **ulama** | the class of scholars specialising in Islamic law |

# Further reading

*The Travels of Ibn Battuta* by Ibn Battuta. Translated by
Tim Mackintosh-Smith. Picador. Probably the best
modern translation and abridgement of the *Rihla*.

*Ibn Battuta: Travels in Asia and Africa 1325-1354* by Ibn
Battuta. Translated by H.A.R. Gibb. Routledge. The
classic, complete translation by Gibb.

*The Adventures of Ibn Battuta: A Muslim Traveler of the 14th
Century* by Ross E. Dunn. University of California
Press. Excellent account of Ibn Battuta's travels, placing
them into historical context.

*Travels with a Tangerine: A Journey in the Footnotes of Ibn
Battutah* by Tim Mackintosh-Smith. John Murray. A
fine modern travel writer retraces the first part of Ibn
Battuta's adventures.

*The Hall of a Thousand Columns: Hindustan to Malabar
with Ibn Battutah* by Tim Mackintosh-Smith. John
Murray. Mackintosh-Smith continues in the tracks of
Ibn Battuta.

*Landfalls: On the Edge of Islam from Zanzibar to the
Alhambra* by Tim Mackintosh-Smith. John Murray.
The final volume of Mackintosh-Smith's retracing of
Ibn Battuta's voyages.

# Index

# The author

Edoardo Albert is a writer and historian. He has written about the first Anglo-Saxon kings, the last man to know everything and swords. Quite a lot about swords. To find out more, visit his website, www.edoardoalbert.com, like him on Facebook, www.facebook.com/EdoardoAlbert. writer, or follow him on Twitter @EdoardoAlbert. He enjoys hearing from readers.